Mindfulness & Minimalist Budget

© Copyright 2017 by Charlie Mason - All rights reserved.

The following eBook is reproduced below with the goal of providing information that is as accurate and as reliable as possible. Regardless, purchasing this eBook can be seen as consent to the fact that both the publisher and the author of this book are in no way experts on the topics discussed within, and that any recommendations or suggestions made herein are for entertainment purposes only. Professionals should be consulted as needed before undertaking any of the action endorsed herein.

This declaration is deemed fair and valid by both the American Bar Association and the Committee of Publishers Association and is legally binding throughout the United States.

Furthermore, the transmission, duplication or reproduction of any of the following work, including precise information, will be considered an illegal act, irrespective whether it is done electronically or in print. The legality extends to creating a secondary or tertiary copy of the work or a recorded copy and is only allowed with an express written consent of the Publisher. All additional rights are reserved.

The information in the following pages is broadly considered to be a truthful and accurate account of facts, and as such any inattention, use or misuse of the information in question by the reader will render any resulting actions solely under their purview. There are no scenarios in which the publisher or the original author of this work can be in any fashion deemed liable for any hardship or damages that may befall them after undertaking information described herein.

Additionally, the information found on the following pages is intended for informational purposes only and should thus be considered, universal. As befitting its nature, the information presented is without assurance regarding its continued validity or interim quality. Trademarks that mentioned are done without written consent and can in no way be considered an endorsement from the trademark holder.

Table of Contents

Mindfulness 6
- Introduction 7
- 1. What Is OCD? 8
- 2. Deep Breathing 10
- 3. Take Notice of Your Surroundings 12
- 4. Slow Down 14
- 5. Meditate 16
- 6. Develop Concentration 18
- 7. Be Kind to Yourself 20
- 8. Journaling 22
- 9. Counseling 24
- 10. Don't Be Judgmental 26
- 10. Let Go and Have Fun 28
- Conclusion 30

Minimalist Budget: 32
- Introduction 33
- Chapter 1 - The Psychology of Purchasing 34
- Chapter 2 - How to Ignore Advertisements 38
- Chapter 3 - How to Get Over Compulsive 41
- Chapter 4 - Increase Your Self-Confidence 44
- Chapter 5 - Improve Your Spending Habits 48

Chapter 6 - Savings Strategy to Get Out of Debt......... 50

Chapter 7 - Money Management Guide.......................... 52

Chapter 8 - Feel Financially Secure Every Day 54

Conclusion: 56

Mindfulness

Top 10 Tips to Overcoming Obsessions and Compulsions Using Mindfulness

Introduction

Twenty years ago, the idea of being mindful was largely relegated to Eastern religions and New Age ideas. Nowadays, however, researchers and the general population are both finding more and more that mindfulness has incredible benefits at helping people deal with the stress and anxiety of daily life. It can actually even help to rewire your brain to be more calm and optimistic!

This book is specifically about mindfulness as a way of helping people who suffer from OCD. Because for many people, OCD is associated with stress and anxiety, and mindfulness can help alleviate some of the symptoms. This book will give you 10 different tips at becoming mindful, as well as some practical steps that you can take towards implementing those tips in your daily life. The intended result is that you will be able to gain more control over your symptoms of OCD and be empowered to live a more productive, fulfilling life.

1. WHAT IS OCD?

Obsessive-Compulsive Disorder, commonly known as OCD, is a mental disorder in which someone feels constant urges to clean something, repeat certain routines or rituals, or have repetitive thought patterns. The person may wash his or her hands repetitively, constantly check the oven knobs to make sure that they are off, constantly check the doors to make sure that they are locked, or constantly count things. For many who suffer from OCD, it has interfered with their daily lives because dealing with the compulsions takes up an hour or more of their time every day, and the repetitive thoughts associated with the disorder keep them from experiencing meaningful relationships and fully engaging in their activities of daily living. In extreme cases, the symptoms can be so damaging that the person is led to contemplate or even attempt suicide.

While the cause of the disorder is unknown, for many people, it is associated with anxiety and stress. A large number of people who have it have experienced a major traumatic event, particularly child abuse but also events such as the death of a loved one or a major car accident. Other causes may include infection and genetics. Half of all cases of OCD present before the age of 20 and development of symptoms after the age of 35 is extremely rare. Worldwide, about 1% of the population is believed to be affected with OCD every year, and approximately 2-3% of the population is affected at some point in their lifetimes.

Treatments for OCD include medication, such as selective serotonin reuptake inhibitors, as well as Cognitive Behavioral Therapy (CBT) to help people learn to deal with the intrusive, repetitive thoughts. One particularly successful method of treating OCD is learning mindfulness. Mindfulness is the practice of being fully aware of what is going on both around and inside of you so that you can distinguish your own negative thoughts from what is actually happening, separate your own feelings from the facts, and not feel the need to treat every thought you have as if you are actually facing a threat.

2. DEEP BREATHING

One of the most beneficial yet most overlooked methods of practicing mindfulness is to engage in deep breathing exercises. You don't have to sit in a lotus position humming "ohm," but if you feel so compelled, then do so. All that you need to do is sit up straight (make sure that your back is as straight as possible), breathe in, and breathe out. Take 10 seconds to inhale and 20 seconds to exhale. Practice this simple exercise for two minutes a day.

The benefits of engaging in deep breathing are so immense that one must wonder why this simple exercise is so often overlooked. One reason why is that it naturally triggers the parasympathetic nervous system, which promotes a relaxation response. It actually causes your body to physiologically relax! Many diseases, including OCD, are either directly or indirectly correlated with stress, and most of us lead busy and stressful lives. Deep breathing is a way to make you consciously slow down and take notice of what is going on inside of you. By being aware of what you are thinking and feeling, you can get a better grasp of what are your own thoughts, which may be distortions of reality, and what is actually going on around you.

One reason why your body starts to feel tense whenever you feel anxious is because you are not breathing deeply. When you breathe shallowly, your body does not receive the oxygen that it needs and is therefore unable to properly fuel your cells. Breathing deeply gets all of the oxygen your body needs to every part of it, enabling your contracted muscles to relax. This response is crucial to helping you get control over the symptoms of OCD. You cannot simply think your way out of OCD; if you could, you probably would have found much relief from your symptoms by now. Your body needs to be in tune with your thoughts; if your body is out of sync because it does not have proper oxygen, you will be unable to control the impulses of OCD. However, having an adequate supply of oxygen will enable your relaxed mind to ward off some of the impulses.

Breathing deeply can even detoxify your body. One of the primary toxins in your body is carbon dioxide; if your lungs are compromised by shallow breathing, you will not be able to expel it correctly and it will build up. Getting rid of toxins like carbon dioxide will allow your mind and body to function better.

Another benefit of deep breathing is that it can even relieve pain and increase happiness. This is because it stimulates the release of hormones such as serotonin, the "happiness hormone." Serotonin naturally alleviates stress and anxiety, so stimulating its release is an ideal way to help you control your OCD.

So take two minutes now and breathe in deeply for 10 seconds. Then exhale for 20 seconds. Do it again a few times. You will notice that you start to feel calm and relaxed after just a couple of minutes.

3. TAKE NOTICE OF YOUR SURROUNDINGS

Many of us have busy lives that we do not take the time to stop and smell the roses and we don't even notice that there are roses! If we do, we don't think about whether they are red, yellow, or pink, or about how pretty they are. We simply are not aware of what is going on around us. One way to practice mindfulness is to stop and take notice of your surroundings.

Look around you for a minute. How many colors do you see? Do you see the color brown? In how many places do you see brown? What about red? Pink? Blue? What is your favorite color? How many times do you see it? Notice how you just slowed your brain down so that it is no longer racing. Do you feel less anxious yet, at least a little bit?

Breathe in deeply through your nose. What do you smell? Coffee? Your coworker's perfume? Something cooking? Does it smell pleasant? Does the smell make you happy or bring to mind any memories? Stop and think about the smells around you. Experience them. Breathe in and out deeply. Are you feeling calmer? Good.

How much time do you spend eating your food? If you are like most people in the modern world, you probably don't spend much time eating. After all, you have to get back to work. There are so many things that you need to do in just a small amount of time! Stop. That kind of thinking provokes anxiety and will trigger OCD symptoms. Try to spend more time eating. Take time to notice what you are eating. How does your food smell? What does it look like? Take each bite slowly. What does it taste like? What is its texture? How do the different textures that you are eating interact with each other? Do you like the textures? Take a sip of something after every three bites. Enjoy your food and fully experience it.

What is that that you hear? Is it a fly or mosquito buzzing around your head? Is it the overhead light making a crackling sound? Is it a conversation going on in the next cubicle? Is it the sound of rain? Are you listening to music? Take a minute and listen to it. No, really listen to it. Pay attention to it. Be aware of the sounds around you and where they are coming from.

Are you sitting at a desk right now? Maybe you are sitting outside in a chair or are relaxing on the sofa. Take a minute and feel it. Run your hands along your desk. What does it feel like?

You should feel more aware of your surroundings by now. Being aware of your surroundings helps you separate your own intrusive thoughts from what is going.

4. SLOW DOWN

Many people are convinced that they have to fill every minute of every day with some kind of activity. As a result, their brains never slow down and they are never able to enter a state of relaxation. They even have impaired sleep because their brains are always wired. Constantly being on the go can actually trick your brain into believing that there is a threat, and your brain has a built-in defense to threats: the fight-or-flight response. Adrenaline and cortisol get released into your body, fueling even more stress and making you feel that you have to work harder and do more. Being too busy can actually trigger your brain to respond as if you are under a threat. There is actually great value in simply slowing down.

Slowing down means that you don't feel the need to fill up every single minute of every single day with activities. You can simply let yourself be. Sit outside on the grass and enjoy the feeling of it on your feet. Enjoy the way that the sun shines on your skin; fully experience the warmth of it. Go play with your dog. Push a kid on the swing. Do something that you enjoy rather than something that feels productive and busy. Too often, we feel that we have to be busy in order for life to be meaningful. However, that is simply not true. Meaning is found in the moments when we slow down and enjoy our surroundings and the people that we are with.

How many times a day do you check your phone? How many times an hour? How long can you go without checking your email or text messages? This is something to be aware of. Constantly checking your phone distracts you from mindfulness because it wires your brain to believe that if you aren't being productive, you are wasting time. Put your phone away and go for a walk. The world can wait. You need to take care of your own self and your own needs.

What keeps you from slowing down? What makes you believe that you have to be constantly on the go? Do you ever feel that your mind is racing? Does being busy fuel anxious thoughts?

Now take an hour to just relax and let yourself be. Step away from electronics, including the television, and connect with yourself and your environment. How do you feel? Is your mind slowing down? What is happening to your anxious thoughts?

Try to take an hour every day to slow down and just let yourself be. Don't let yourself become distracted and overwhelmed by everything that you think you need to do. Stop and smell the roses.

5. MEDITATE

You've already looked at the benefits of deep breathing, being aware of your surroundings, and slowing down. Tying all of those things together is the art of meditation. Meditation is when you allow your mind to slow down focus on something. If you have ever been kept awake at night by an anxious thought that keeps turning around in your head and that you can't distance yourself from, then you are actually meditating on that anxious thought. However, that kind of meditation is negative. Positive meditation is when you intentionally focus on good or positive things and don't concern yourself with the negative thoughts that try to invade.

Many religions have their own meditative practices that are designed to enhance the individual's spirituality or connection with his or her own spirit. Kabbalah, the Jewish mystical tradition, has meditative practices designed to lift the individual from his or her own daily struggles and into the cognizance of the Eternal One. Christianity adopted some Kabbalistic practices, which are used by Christians to meditate on the Divine. Islam, especially the Sufi branch, also has meditative practices. Some religions, such as Hinduism, Sikhism, and Jainism, find meditation to be so intrinsic to an individual's spiritual well-being that it is a prescribed part of daily life. If you associate yourself with any religion, a good place to start is to learn about what your religion says about meditation and how you should practice it.

If you are not religious and are not interested in what these different religions say about meditation, you can still learn to meditate. Sit up straight and close your eyes. Keep your posture as perfect as you can so that you can breathe in fully and deeply. Inhale for 10 seconds and exhale for 20 seconds. Continue inhaling and exhaling in this manner while you do one of the following:

1. Tell yourself positive things. You are a good person. You are aware of your surroundings and you are mindful of what is going on inside of you. You can overcome your OCD so that it no longer dominates your life.

2. Focus on something positive. This can be an image of the ocean, a favorite childhood memory, or something entirely innocuous, like a door or window frame.

Remain in this state for as long as you can. If you can only meditate for a couple of minutes at first, that's fine. Keep practicing meditation every day and try to remain a bit longer each time.

At first, you may find that you are distracted by things that need to be done. If you try to meditate first thing in the morning, you may be so distracted by the need to get to work on time that you aren't able to meditate successfully. If that's the case, try to find a time that works for you, when you won't be so distracted.

The point of meditation is to empty your mind of negative thoughts so that it can be filled with positivity. Meditation is actually a powerful tool that can rewire your brain to think more positively.

6. DEVELOP CONCENTRATION

Many of us live lives that are so busy that we don't know the value of concentration; and not only that, we don't even know how to concentrate. When was the last time you were able to work for two hours straight without having to check your phone or email? Your answer to that question should give you an indication of how well you are able to concentrate.

A huge part of the problem is that many people actually see distraction as a good thing. They sit on a park bench and stare at their phones instead of watching the ducks in the pond. Many people can't even get through a meal with their friends and/or family without their phones! Be honest with yourself: How much is your phone keeping you from being able to concentrate on your own life?

Being able to concentrate is actually the cornerstone of mindfulness. If you cannot focus on the task at hand because you are so distracted, then there is very little room for you to be aware of your own thoughts, your feelings, the people around you and your environment.

Here are some tips for helping you to develop your ability to concentrate.

> 1. Turn off and tune out all distractions. If you are used to listening to music or keeping the television on, turn those things off. Put your cell phone on silent or off and tuck it away. Close out all of your internet tabs except for the one that you are currently using.
>
> 2. Practice deep breathing and meditation every day. The powerful effect that these exercises have on your mind can

help you train it to tune out distractions and focus on the task at hand.

3. Exercise. Exercise helps stimulate the release of hormones that will help you concentrate. It also burns adrenaline and cortisol out of your system, both of which can be a deterrent to concentration.

4. Only try to do one thing at a time. Our society values multitasking, but multitasking is really a myth. You can't focus on two things at once. What actually happens when you try to multitask is your brain constantly jumps between tasks, causing you to do everything more inefficiently. So think about what is the thing that you need to be working on right now, and just do that one thing. Write down everything else that you need to do so that you don't forget, and get to those things in their proper time.

When you are able to concentrate better, those impulsive thoughts associated with OCD will have less room to invade your mind. You will be more focused on what you are actually doing and less concerned about going to wash your hands or make sure that the door is locked. You will also have the tremendous satisfaction of getting your job done well.

7. BE KIND TO YOURSELF

Many of us lead incredibly busy, hectic lives because we are constantly trying to please others. We work so hard to please the boss. We throw a party to please our friends. We cook dinner to please our families. One effect of anxiety is that you can become so tied up in pleasing other people that you don't recognize or appreciate the need to please yourself. If you do, you may talk yourself out of it by saying that you don't have the time or there are too many other things and people that you need to take care of.

However, there is great value in being kind to yourself. Go to the salon and get a manicure and pedicure. Get your hair done. Cook your favorite dinner. Eat dessert without apologizing. Go to the park. Go to the ball game. Rent the movie that you've been wanting to see. Go out with your friends and do something so fun that it's ridiculous.

When you are kind to yourself, you actually increase your own self-esteem and self-awareness. You become more aware of the things that you like and the things that may irritate you or set you off. You may be able to find the things that trigger your compulsions and cause you to have repetitive, negative thoughts. By engaging in the things that you like, you can rewire your brain to actually be more positive. It will release those positive hormones, like serotonin, and even cleanse itself of toxins.

The corollary of being kind to yourself is allowing other people to be kind to you. Let your friends, family, and coworkers show that they appreciate you. If someone wants to give you a gift, don't feel that you have to give one in reciprocity. Many times, we allow ourselves to feel guilty when someone does something kind. That is a mistake. Think of what motive you had last time you did something kind for someone. Was it to get something in return, or was it because you just wanted to be nice? If a friend wants to be nice and buy you dinner, don't feel that you have to do the same. If you want to, great. But don't feel obligated to.

What is your guilty pleasure? Why does it make you feel guilty? What is something that you would really like to do at the end of the day? What keeps you from doing it? How can you deal with the obstacles and anxieties that keep you from being kind to yourself and doing the things that you enjoy?

Be mindful of the things that you enjoy and how they make you feel. Be mindful of why you do or don't allow yourself to partake of these activities. And most importantly, be kind to yourself.

8. JOURNALING

Journaling is a great way to become aware of your own thoughts and feelings. Knowing yourself — being self-aware by understanding your thoughts, actions, motivations, and feelings — is a powerful key to being mindful. Journaling is a great way to help you become more self-aware.

One important aspect of mindfulness in regards to OCD is being able to understand what your triggers are. In other words, what are some things that cause you to have compulsive thoughts? Maybe something that is seemingly innocuous, like a clock or a set of keys, is connected with a particularly stressful or traumatic memory. You may not realize that those things are actually triggers.

Journaling can help you identify your triggers. If you notice yourself having a lot of compulsive thoughts that you just can't seem to get rid of, take out your journal and start writing about what is going on. What exactly is going on around you? What are you thinking? What are you feeling? Who is involved in the situation? What are those people saying or doing? After a while, you may notice a pattern in what you are writing. You may see that certain things are making you particularly nervous or anxious and setting off compulsive thoughts.

Journaling can also help you put some of your nervousness and anxiety to rest. Instead of tossing the same idea around your head for hours and hours, keeping yourself awake at night, write it down. Write down everything that is causing you stress, how that stress feels, and how it impacts your life. You may feel a tremendous sense of release just by writing these things down. Writing out your thoughts has actually been shown to have a healing effect on the mind and body.

There are other ways that journaling can help bring you into a state of mindfulness. It brings you from being annoyed or distracted by your surroundings to helping you become in touch with your own thoughts and feelings about what is going on. It can help in making you aware of your own likes, dislikes, and what you ultimately want out of life.

Here are some ideas that you can journal about.

1. What is something that happened today that made me happy?
2. What is something that happened today that made me feel an unpleasant emotion (pain, anger, sadness, anxiety, etc.)?
3. What compulsive thoughts did I have today? What did I do with those compulsive thoughts? What was the result?
4. What is something that no one else knows about me?

While you can certainly use your computer to journal, there is actually a therapeutic benefit that comes from writing things out on paper. Go on, try it. Get a notebook and pen and start writing. You may find that your mind is instantly set at ease.

9. COUNSELING

There are some counseling methods that have been developed specifically for people who suffer from OCD. One of them is Cognitive Behavioral Therapy (CBT) which teaches people to be aware of their own thought patterns so that they can change them. It is a very effective way for people to develop mindfulness, particularly for people with anxiety and OCD.

The model that CBT uses is that our actions are motivated by our thoughts, which are heavily influenced by our core beliefs. Our core beliefs are basically what we believe about ourselves and the world around us. If our core beliefs say that we are good, valuable, strong, worthy, we can do great things, and our lives matter, then the thoughts that we have will generally be positive and pleasant. We will be able to feel good about ourselves and in return, we can be good to other people. If our core beliefs say that we are insignificant, incapable, unworthy, and life is unfair and that the world is a harsh and demanding place, then negative, anxious thoughts will follow. Those thoughts could be why you have the compulsions that you have.

CBT helps you become aware of the negative thoughts that you have, as well as the core beliefs that shape them so that you can work to change them. Changing negative thoughts to positive ones can have a significant impact on decreasing anxiety and stress and helping you live a happy, meaningful, and purposeful life. By decreasing the stress, you may be able to simultaneously decrease the compulsive thoughts that have been plaguing you. CBT has actually been shown to reduce compulsions by up to 70%. Imagine how much of your life you could get back if you had 70% fewer compulsions.

CBT is not the only type of counseling that can help people with

OCD. There is also DBT, or Dialectical Behavioral Therapy, which functions under a model very similar to the CBT model. In addition to helping you change your core beliefs, DBT helps you gain tools to deal with some of the difficulties that you may face, especially your triggers.

Going to a counselor can be scary and intimidating. If you are worried about what others will think, remember that you are under no obligation to let anybody know. The thought of opening up to somebody that you don't know about all of your fears and anxieties can itself be very anxious. Keep in mind that counselors trained in conducting CBT, DBT, and other forms of therapy. They go through a rigorous process to become licensed. They also receive ongoing training so that they can be aware of the newest research and approaches.

Some counselors have different specialties, such as grief counseling or anger management. Look for a therapist who is specially trained in treating OCD. He or she will probably have both training and experience in helping people like you find freedom from their compulsions.

10. DON'T BE JUDGMENTAL

If you suffer from OCD, the odds are that you are blaming yourself for something that might happen in the future. You probably judge yourself. Very harshly. A lot. However, part of being mindful is accepting your present reality without being judgmental, either of yourself, others, or of the things that are happening. This means that whatever happens, you aren't blaming yourself or the people around you. Yes, maybe you could have done things differently and seen different results. However, you need to recognize that you are not the problem.

Forgive yourself. You are not perfect, and that's OK. You have probably made some mistakes, some of them pretty big. You have probably hurt other people and also hurt yourself. Guess what? So has everyone else on the planet. Instead of being harsh and judgmental on yourself, you need to forgive yourself for not being perfect. This means that you accept yourself just the way you are, your OCD, and all. While you certainly want to minimize the mistakes that you make, you need to recognize that everyone makes mistakes. While some mistakes really aren't OK, and maybe you have made some that aren't OK, you are OK just the way you are. You don't need to change. Love yourself just the way you are.

Forgive others. This one is easier said than done because if you are like anyone else on the planet, you have probably been hurt extensively by the people around you. You may feel that you can never trust another person again. Something that someone else did to you may actually be the reason you have anxiety and OCD. However, forgiveness is the only way to find freedom from what happened. A wise person said that forgiveness is setting a prisoner free and then finding that the prisoner was you.
Forgiving someone doesn't mean that you minimize or forget

what that person did. It means that you stare hard at the reality of what happened, acknowledging it fully, and then break ties with it. The process is not simple. It's actually a very, very hard thing to do. You may not be ready to forgive, but maybe you are ready to be ready to forgive. Freeing yourself from all the grudges you have towards your enemy, your life, and even to yourself will give you a long lasting peace. A religious clergy person, therapist, or trusted friend can help you through the process of forgiving those who have hurt you.

Separate yourself from your OCD. You are not your OCD. It is something that you have to contend with. You have to learn how to cope with it, and you are learning to cope with it because you have read this far in this book. However, it does not define you. It does not make you the wonderful person that you are.

10. Let Go and Have Fun

While for some people having fun is the air that they breathe, for many people with OCD, it can actually be quite a challenge. After all, how are you supposed to stop worrying about the oven knobs or front door? What should you do when the anxious, repetitive thoughts arise? What if people find out that you're crazy?

Relax. You aren't crazy. However, if you have been suffering from OCD for a while, your brain is probably wired in such a way that having fun may actually be a challenge. Loosening up is hard to do when you have intense anxiety and are constantly worrying.

However, getting out and having fun can be a powerful tool in dealing with your anxiety. Maybe you feel like you are not allowed to have fun, or that you are doomed to be miserable. And who are you to mess with fate? Sometimes, just getting out of the house is an achievement. While it will probably be hard at first, your brain will release the hormones that will naturally cause you to be happy and banish some of your anxiety.

If you find that you are too anxious to leave the house, consider having someone come over for a visit. You can have dinner together and then watch a movie. You may worry about whether or not the other person will actually have fun. If that's the case, let the other person pick out what movie to watch and/or what to eat. Be kind to yourself and don't try to do more than you are able.

Before you go out or have someone come over, you may need to prepare yourself by practicing some mindfulness. Start by doing some deep-breathing exercises. Meditate to help you banish your anxious thoughts and replace them with positive ones. After all, you really are going to have a good time and enjoy yourself! Are you feeling stressed about going out? Write in your journal about how you feel. What about going out makes you feel stressed? Why do you think you have that trigger? What can you do to help release the anxiety so that you can enjoy yourself as much as possible?

For those who are intentionally self-aware, going out and having fun can actually be the epitome of mindfulness. You intentionally experience things that you enjoy and give you pleasure. You relish the experience of pleasure by appreciating every moment, all of the people that you are with, what you are doing, and the opportunity to have fun. If you have OCD and are working on being mindful, you can intentionally create memories that you can look back on and relive in your mind when you are feeling particularly stressed or anxious.

CONCLUSION

Mindfulness is for everyone. It enables us to slow down and actually experience our lives rather than racing through them at breakneck speed. It keeps us from judging ourselves and the people around us and helps us to accept things as they are. You probably know plenty of people who can benefit from that kind of outlook.

For people with OCD, there are particular benefits to mindfulness that can actually decrease the symptoms and compulsions and help them live a more meaningful, satisfying life. If you have OCD, you can follow the above guidelines for mindfulness to help you decrease your anxiety and find relief from your compulsions. Mindfulness seems like a rather easy thing.

So easy that one might think it is mindless! However, nothing could be further from the truth. Disciplining yourself to do deep-breathing is hard. Meditating is hard. It means deliberately focusing your attention away from the negative thoughts that probably fill your mind nearly every minute of every day. Journaling is relaxing and healing, but no one said that it is easy. Slowing down your busy life, especially when you have filled it with busyness to avoid your pain and anxiety, is hard.

Turning off your cell phone is hard. And forgiving people who have hurt you, truly facing the pain that you have experienced and relinquishing your right to judge the person who inflicted it on you, there is nothing easy about that. These are all habits that you have to intentionally form. They don't just happen.

You may need to find a professional therapist to help guide you through the process of becoming mindful and thereby decreasing your symptoms of OCD. You will probably also want to find people, such as friends and family, who can support you. Maybe they will want to join in on your journey to mindfulness and you can hold each other accountable for practicing mindfulness techniques every day. The journey will be hard. However, the end results will be well worth the effort. You will find freedom from many of your compulsions and be able to get your life back.

Minimalist Budget:

Simple Strategies On How to Save More and Become Financially Secure.

Introduction

I want to thank you and congratulate you for downloading this book!

This book contains proven steps and strategies on how to save more and become financially secure. Are you one of those people who cannot leave a shopping mall or an online retail store without purchasing anything? Do you find yourself out of money long before your next paycheck? Does your budget seem so stretched out yet you still seem to lack so many things? If you answered yes to all these questions and are looking for ways to make your paycheck last longer, the solution is to adopt the concept of a minimalist budget. This concept will help you understand the reasons why you spend, provide you with ideas on how curb your impulse buying tendencies and save you money. It will show you how much better your life can become even without spending a lot of money. You will also get tips on how to save more and improve your spending habits. This book will help you become more in control of your money and your finances and show you the many money saving tips that will help you save more and spend less. If you're ready to start saving, turn to the next page and see what's in store for you.

Thanks again for downloading this book, I hope you enjoy it!

Chapter 1 - The Psychology of Purchasing

There are many reasons why people buy things, but psychology will tell you that there are 4 most basic psychological behaviors that help you understand why you buy what you buy. These four factors according to psychologists also predict the things that you will buy in the future.

Factor #1 – Satisfaction of Needs

This is the most basic reason why people purchase stuff - because of a need that they have to fulfill. Most of the things that people buy are bought because there is some intrinsic need that they have to fulfill. Needs can be classified as basic or complex.
Basic needs are those that fulfill your base requirements. These base requirements are often associated to physical needs. Things that your body needs to function normally are called basic needs. Examples of basic needs are food, water, and shelter.
Complex needs are those that fulfill your emotional, spiritual, and other forms of non-physical need. These can include having friends, belonging to a group, or taking on a hobby that relaxes you. Complex needs sometimes overlap with the other need psychological reasons why people buy things.

Factor #2 – Attention and Perception

This psychological factor in purchasing is the thing that advertisers and marketing teams have influence over. These two go hand in hand because perception is often dependent on attention.

An advertiser's goal is to get the attention of the customers long enough for them to build a perception on the product that they are selling. Perception can be favorable or not. The goal is always

to create a favorable one so people will want to buy the product.
To capture the buyer's attention, advertisers make sure that their advertisement is catchy, witty, and truly attention grabbing. Some advertisers use special effects, unusual ideas, and gimmicks just to get the buyer to look at their product or make the buyer aware that such a product exists.

Once the buyer's attention is caught, he can form a perception on the type of product being sold. If he finds that the product makes him feel good or fulfills his needs, the buyer will more often than not, buy that item. If he does not feel that the item is not going to be of any use to him or if he dislikes the message that the advertisement is sending, the buyer will not likely want to buy that product.

Most advertisers know that perception can be altered. That is why they use a tactic called repetition and distortion.

Repetition is when they keep showing the product in different channels where a buyer will be most likely to see it. These channels include TV, print, and online. The more a person sees these repetitive advertisements, the more the products stick to their minds. This makes it easier for them to recall the marketing message when they are faced with this product in a supermarket for example. The familiarity makes a person more enticed to buy it.

Distortion is a form of manipulation of the person's perception to make the product more favorable in the eyes of the buyer. A good example of distortion is making something that is often perceived as a bad thing look good. A gun, for example, is something that people would associate with death or as weapons that can harm people. But gun manufacturers would market it as a form of protection or something that can keep the persons you love safe.

Factor #3 – Knowledge and Conditioning

To buy a product, most people will do their research about that particular product. This is true for items that the person has never used before or items that are expensive. An average person will find out everything he can about the product before making that purchase.

Some people are influenced by knowledge about the product as provided by other people. If the knowledge about the product is not good, an advertiser's job is to condition the person to change his perception by presenting him with a different set of knowledge that will appeal to him before he can be convinced to buy the product.

Knowledge and learnings from other people's experience also influence the way people buy things. This is the reason why people turn to reviews, unboxing, samples, and try-before-you-buy promos before they buy into what the advertisers are saying. Reviews show the buyer an actual encounter with the product without buying the product.

Factor #4 – Beliefs, Cultures, and Attitudes

A big factor in the psychology of purchasing is a person's set of beliefs, cultures, and attitudes. A person can be influenced into buying something because it is something that has been inculcated in his system even before he has formed his perception about a particular product. It is something that has become a habit and permanent thing in a person's life.

A good example of this is when a person does not buy pork because his belief dictates that pork is an animal that is associated with a scavenger that eats dirt and muck. People with this belief are taught early on in their life that pork is dirty so they avoid it at all costs.

These are just some of the most common psychological factors that can explain why people buy or don't buy a particular item. There are more reasons that are often far more complex than these four. These complex reasons are often combinations of these four basic influencers.

Chapter 2 - How to Ignore Advertisements

Advertisements are created mainly to give customers an idea of what products are available in the market and to entice them to buy these products. They would be shown on TV, print, and on the internet. Big companies pay top dollar to get the best time slot on TV or the billboard spot along the busiest roads. They also pour huge amounts of money on marketing teams and creatives in order to get ahead of the competition.

Unless you live under a rock, you cannot truly escape advertising. It comes from so many different channels that it's hard to really block them off completely. But there is a way to ignore them. Some of the most effective ways are detailed here:

1. Lessen Your Exposure – TV and the internet are some of the most common places where advertising thrives. Lessen your exposure to these channels and you lessen your exposure to advertisements. When watching TV, for example, you can try standing up and doing other things during commercial breaks instead of sitting through the ads and mindlessly watching them. Watching commercials make the products repetitive and easy to recall to make you more susceptible to impulse buys.

2. You can use commercial breaks to go to the bathroom, do some sit ups, talk with the person you are sitting beside, or check your email. Put the TV on mute while the commercials are on to ensure that you don't hear anything.

3. Adblocking Software – if you must use the internet (as almost everyone does), you can find a good adblocking software that can filter advertisements so you don't have to see them or see them as often. These adblockers often

come with a price. Choose one that will fit your needs and your budget.

4. Use Subscription Services – Some subscription services such as Netflix allow you to watch TV without commercials interrupting you every 10 seconds. You will need to pay for these services on a monthly basis but you can be assured that you need not see an ad while you are enjoying your show.

5. Increase your Knowledge – the more you know about a product, the less likely you are to acknowledge the promos and gimmicks that other advertisements are parading. You can ignore an advertisement better if you know a product inside and out. Knowing the ins and outs of your favorite products make you less susceptible to buying a new product just because it has the words NEW and IMPROVED stamped in front of its packaging.

6. Avoid Window Shopping – for some, this may be hard to do. But avoiding the shopping mall or the online shop altogether is one of the best ways to ignore advertisements. Instead of window shopping, use your time for more productive yet equally enjoyable activities. Write on your journal, go for a jog, read a book, or take up a new hobby.

7. Learn to be Content with What You Have - One of the reasons why advertisements work is that they would always try to convince the customers that they need that particular product in their life in order to live better. But when a person is content with what he has, he becomes less inclined to buy that product. If your phone is still working and serving its purpose, for example, and you are content with its performance, you will not think about replacing it as soon as the new model comes out. You will

not want the new features as much because you are satisfied with your phone.

8. Be Alert – be wary of advertisements that offer miracle cures and unbelievable claims. These advertisements are often presented in the form of infomercials. Although their claims border on the impossible, all the information, research findings, expert opinion, and testimonials that they put in their infomercials convince consumers of their product's effectiveness. Be wary of these tactics and do not immediately fall for these false advertisements.

9. Get Rid of Temptation – Don't take flyers handed out at the malls, get rid of spam and junk mail, and do not subscribe to retail newsletter or text alerts. These tell you more about new products that you can spend on. The less you know, the better you will be at not buying anything. Besides, if you really need something, you will definitely go out and search for it. You do not have to yield to the marketers when they tell you that you need their products.

You may find it hard to do these things at first especially if your habits include the activities you need to avoid i.e. watching TV mindlessly. But with practice and a good amount of willpower, you can become an expert at ignoring advertisements. Keep practicing and soon it will become second nature to you that you don't notice yourself doing it anymore.

Chapter 3 - How to Get Over Compulsive Spending Habits

Compulsive spending as defined by many psychological experts is a human behavior wherein a person would put a huge amount of time and effort in buying things to a point that it strains or impairs his life and relationships.

This manner of spending is considered a psychological problem that often requires intervention and help from qualified therapists. It is sometimes considered as a form of addiction because a person experiences a natural high whenever he acquires an item. That high can be addicting to the point that a person loses money and property and severs relationships.

The most common effect of compulsive shopping for some people is the feeling of happiness. Compulsive spenders feel happy every time they purchase something. But they instantly regret it because it usually eventually leads to getting deep in debt. They tend to buy stuff whenever they are depressed or sad to make them happy. Their shopping habits get out of hand and sometimes lead to disagreements and discord between them and the people they love. Rifts start to form until families are torn apart all because of this addiction.

To help you get over your compulsive spending habits, here are some of the most effective ways.

Cut Up Your Credit Cards – some people don't see credit cards as harmful because they don't see actual money being exchanged between them and the retail shop. This gives you the illusion that you are not really spending any money. You become more confident at spending because you see that you still have a balance on your bank account. But when the bill comes, you will realize that you have more purchases than money in the bank.

The best way to ensure that you don't spend unnecessarily you should know where your money is going. It is best for you to spend using cash. When you see your money dwindling, you will be less likely to keep buying.

Bring Exact Amounts – you know how much the bus fares are. Your lunch money or food allowance for the day should also be budgeted so you know your limit. Bring only that much money for the day so you will not be tempted to buy something while you are cruising along the mall.
If you are afraid that you will be caught in an emergency, you can bring enough money to get you home, but make sure that it's not in the same pocket or wallet as your spending money so do not "accidentally" spend it. Use it for actual emergencies only.

Track the Things That You Buy – when you track the things that you purchase, you are less likely to buy duplicate things. It also helps you become more conscious of your spending. Tracking your spending will help you understand where your money is going. Make a list using an app or the note function of your phone to make it easy.

Wait Before Buying – Buy an item only after waiting for some time. Around 30 – 60 minutes is a good amount of time to wait. When you see an item that you really want to buy, your body becomes excited and logic often flies out the door. Calm yourself down and walk away from that item. If, after some time, you still cannot forget that item or feel that you still need it, that is the time to buy. Chances are, once you have walked away, your brain has seen the logic and you will realize that you don't need another pink shirt as you already have 10 at home.

Use a List and Stick to It – The supermarket is a prime trap for impulse buys. With so many items around competing for your attention, it's so hard not to give in and pluck them out from the shelves and put them on your cart. But if you have a list and know the exact places to find the items on your list, you are less likely to wander through aisle after aisle of food and grocery items.

Get the Help of a Buddy – Find people whose willpower is stronger than yours and bring them along with you on your shopping trips. They will help remind you of your no buying policy. Just make sure that you adhere to their reminders otherwise it is futile to bring them along if you are just going to ignore their advice.

Do Something Else Every Time You Feel Like Shopping – Go for a walk, exercise, continue your hobby, or sleep. Keep yourself busy so you don't think of shopping.

The key to getting over your compulsive spending is self-control and self-awareness. Once you have control over your urges and are able to channel them to better activities, you are less likely to give in to the call of retail therapy.

Chapter 4 - Increase Your Self-Confidence with Budgeting

Budgeting is an age old practice where people allocate funds for things that they need to purchase or save for. People who budget their money would plan out how the money gets spent so that all bills are taken care of and needs are met. It is here that you take into consideration your income and match it with the things that you need in order to live a comfortable life.

For some people, budgeting is hard especially when their means or sources of income are limited. But with minimalist budgeting, a budget is always possible no matter how small your income is.

What is a Minimalist Budget?

A minimalist, loosely defined, is someone who uses only a few items in his life and does not feel the need to fill it with material things. You'll see minimalists sometimes living with less than 100 items and still they feel happy despite not having what others consider as luxuries in life.

A minimalist budget is something similar. People who are experts at this kind of budget are mostly minimalists by nature. They keep things simple so they don't have to spend as much. They value quality over quantity so their material possessions last longer than most items in a regular person's closet. They are more discerning and are concerned more about durability and longevity rather than popularity and aesthetics.

Minimalist budgets do not always mean that you have to spend less. Most of the items that minimalists purchase are of high quality so it can sometimes be more expensive in the beginning but will also pay off in the end. Buying a high quality product means that they don't have to keep replacing the product over a long time since it is more durable and long wearing.

Improve Your Self-Confidence in Budgeting With These Tips

To truly create a minimalist budget and improve your self-confidence with budgeting, you can try these simple ideas. These will help you manage your spending without making you feel like you are losing out. These will also help you transition into a full pledged minimalist budget:

1. Find out where your money goes – the first thing you need to do is to list down your expenses. Listing down your expenses will help you identify your spending traps. Is it clothes? Is it too much expensive coffee from your local coffee shop? Once you find out where your money traps are, you will be able to consciously avoid them. If you must have a budget for these expenses, you can put a cap or a limit to the amount that you spend.

2. Allocate amounts to more important items first – list down the things that need to be paid and when they are due. Set aside the money for these expenses as soon as you get your income. Make sure that you don't touch that money for other things.

3. Some people use the envelope method where they put the money in different envelopes. When it's time to pay these expenses, they simply take out that particular envelope while the rest remains untouched.

4. Seek the help of everyone in your household – if you are the only one doing the budgeting while the rest of your family are wastrels, you'll end up frustrated and resentful

of everyone around you. Creating a minimalist budget entails the inputs and cooperation of the people around you. You should get them to understand the reason for your budgeting so they don't feel deprived.

5. Compare Brands and Offers – when buying big ticket items, don't just jump at the first opportunity or deal that comes your way. Find out the best deals available before taking the plunge. Check also the payment plan so you are not surprised by the amount that you need to shell out in order to pay the installment or balance.

6. In buying cars for example, you should find out how long the warranties are, what are the inclusions upon purchase and the other important details. Factor in the monthly payments to your budget and see if you need to make cuts to make it work. Don't just buy because the down payments are low. You could end up paying more in monthly installments.

7. Allot an amount for savings – having a nest egg that you never touch is something that can provide you with a feeling of security and safety. It is important to budget for savings so that come rainy day or when faced with tough situations that require cash, you are covered. The general rule is to allot 20% of your income to savings but you can add more if you are able.

8. Know what is available – some people go shopping to buy something only to find that they already have it at home. They end up having multiples of the same products. When you know what you have and don't have, you are not likely to go shopping just because you cannot find it.

9. Budget for incidentals – Emergencies or incidentals can include a car breaking down and sickness or disability. These instances are often not within your control but will

affect your life in a big way. Include these items in you budget so your income or your savings will not take a big blow in case you encounter such instances.

Budgeting gets easier the more you practice it. Be in the habit of budgeting instead of going shopping without a plan. Budgets may feel constraining to some but when you get used to it, you will see that it is always more economical than buying mindlessly. With enough practice, you can become confident in your budgeting abilities and eventually curb your mindless spending tendencies.

Chapter 5 - Improve Your Spending Habits

Now that you know how to budget, it's time to focus on your spending habits. Your spending habits are the things that define how you use your money. Bad spending habits are characterized by impulse buys, buyers regret and increased debt. Good spending habits, on the other hand, help you get out of debt, give you financial freedom and make you feel secure in your future.

To improve your spending habits, you need to know what is triggering them. For some people, they spend more when they feel sad or depressed. Other people feel like spending when they are happy. Again that mood factor comes to mind. This is not the right way to go.

Shopping when you are depressed, sad, or feeling emotional will make it easy for you to spend more. Your mind will reason out that you had a very bad day and that you need something new to keep you happy. This is only temporary happiness. You will feel a high on your purchase but will soon feel buyer's remorse especially when you realize that you cannot afford to pay for that item. You will also feel like you are drowning in debt which will continue the cycle of depression further.

When you are feeling sad, you should avoid going to shopping malls or to places where you will most likely spend money. Go for activities that will take your mind off your sadness. Things like playing with pets at the park, reading a good book, or writing on your journal will occupy you and take your mind off your sadness. These activities are also not that expensive. You can also try doing something productive. Channel your sadness to art and music and create songs or works of art. You'll be able to release your sadness and create something beautiful at the same time.

Another trigger to spending is happiness. Getting that bonus at work for a job well done can make you feel like a one-time millionaire. This usually makes you feel like indulging and spending tons of money to celebrate your success. While there is nothing wrong with celebrating achievements it is also important to note that too much spending will deplete your funds or bonus so you are back to living off paycheck to paycheck. Don't make this mistake and use up all your money in one go. Allocate them to the right channels i.e. savings, expenses, and other important things before using it up celebrating.

When you come across a windfall or cash inflow, the best thing to do to curb spending is to step back and just breathe. The natural high that you feel from receiving the money will wear off eventually and you will feel more in control of your spending habits. You will gain a more reasonable perspective once the initial thrill has gone and will be less likely to spend.

The best time to go shopping is when you are not feeling a lot of tumultuous and extreme emotions that can influence your spending habits. Shop only when you feel level-headed. Most people also suggest shopping after you have eaten because when you are hungry, you are more likely to spend on things to mask the feeling of hunger.

Another way to improve your spending habits is to become aware of yourself. You should know the underlying cause why you are spending more than necessary. When you know the reasons why, you are better able to avoid these causes so you will never feel the need to spend more.

Chapter 6 - Savings Strategy to Get Out of Debt

Debt is something that everyone experiences at some point in life. If you are in a lot of debt because of your spending and you feel like you will never be free of debt, don't despair. There is still a way to get out of it. To help get out of debt, you need to have the right attitude in spending and saving.

When a person's attitude about spending is sound, he is able to control his spending better and walk away from the temptation of purchasing. People without the right attitude towards spending, like those who see spending as something they are entitled to, will find it so hard to stop himself from buying even if he does not have money anymore.

Saving is one of the best ways to get out of debt. But how do people use savings to do this? Aren't you supposed to pay off everything with the money that you have instead of putting it away as savings? Here's how it's done.

Savings, loosely defined, is an amount of money that you put away to use for the rainy days. When your savings is greater than your debt, you feel more secure about your future. To use savings to get out of debt, you will need to diligently put away the same amount or a greater amount of money regularly.

For example, if you are earning $1,000 a month and you have a debt of $60,000. From your monthly income, you allocate the monthly amount for your regular installments to pay off that debt. At the same time, set aside an amount of money to put away as savings. Once you have accumulated enough money as savings, say $10,000, you can put that savings to good use by paying off a big chunk of your debt. Paying off that much will lessen the interest rates because the principal amount has been decreased further.

While accumulating savings may not always be the easiest way to get out of debt especially if you have a lot of expenses, it is still one of the most effective ways. You should try saving any amount of money to later on use for making lump sum payments for your debt. Apply that lump sum to the principal amounts and soon your debts decrease substantially and you will be debt-free sooner than you expect.

Chapter 7 - Money Management Guide

Managing your money is the process of tracking, budgeting, saving, and investing your money. It is the process that describes what you do with the money that you earn to make it grow and earn bigger yields. For some people, managing money comes very easily. These people usually have a very good knowledge about the financial world. For others, money management might just as well be a foreign language that needs to be deciphered using the Rosetta stone.

To manage money effectively, one of the things that you have to do is to embrace living frugally. To live frugally means that you do not live beyond your means. You only spend on necessities and do not indulge in luxuries too often. You don't waste money on non-essential needs. To do this, you need to distinguish which items are wants and which ones are needs. Spend money only on the things that you need and forget about the extras.

Another way for you to manage your money is by planning your expenses. Create a chart or a schedule that will tell you right away the expenses that you need to pay and when they are due. This ensures that you never miss a payment and incur late penalties in the process. An expense planner also allows you to see where your money really goes and which expenses are really eating up a huge chunk of your cash.

Expert money managers don't buy a 5 dollar coffee when he can brew his own coffee at home for less than a dollar per small cup. This is another way to manage your money. Be smart enough to know when where you can save. Money managers know how to identify the parts of their spending that they can do without and cut these effectively. This translates to bigger savings.

Manage your money with sound investments. This may seem easier said than done but it is one of the best and most effective ways to grow and manage your money. When you invest your money, you are not just letting it sit in the bank doing nothing. You are actually using your money to fund projects that will yield dividends and earnings for you. A successful venture will gain you added income in the form of interest rates on your funds.

Chapter 8 - Feel Financially Secure Every Day

To feel financially secure every day means that you do not have to worry about your future finances. Not many people are able to say that they are financially secure because they don't feel like they have done enough to secure a comfortable future. But just because you don't feel financially secure now does not mean that you will never be. Here are some ways to lessen your financial security worries today and in the future:

1. Build up a solid savings account – knowing that you have something tucked away to use in case of emergencies provides you with a feeling of financial security like no other. With a big savings account, you won't feel like you will end up penniless when you grow old and become unable to work for a living.

2. Buy insurance – an insurance policy is another safety net that helps protect you in case of huge money losses. Some insurance policies that you can buy include life policy, disability policy, and retirement.

3. Invest wisely – people who are financially secure don't just feel happy having a huge savings account. They feel more secure when they know that they have invested their money in places that yield bigger rewards. They invest in things that are proven to be money makers.

4. Declutter and live minimally – people with so many things worry about the upkeep and maintenance of their material possessions. These hinder them from feeling like they are in control of their spending. To make sure that you don't spend too much, you should let go of non-essential items and live with just the necessary things. When you have less

material possessions to worry about, you will feel more secure about your future.

5. Save no matter how little amount you can – putting something in your savings account, no matter how small that amount is will still contribute to your financial security. Make it a habit to put in something in your savings.

Conclusion:

Thank you again for downloading this book!

I hope this book was able to help you to understand the reasons why you spend, provide you with ideas on how curb your impulse buying tendencies and save you money. Remember, there are steps that you can do today in order to ensure that you will not have to worry about whether or not you will have enough money during your sunset years. It only takes some discipline in saving more and a whole lot of restraint when it comes to spending.

I only have a SMALL favor that I need from you, do you think you can help me out?

As I'm sure you know reviews are the roots of success on Amazon and as a one man self-publisher, I need as many reviews as I can get. I hope I have landed your 5 star review (:

Click the country you are from to leave me a review (even a few words will mean a lot to me and it will only take less than 2 minutes)

- I am from USA
- I am from UK
- I am from another country

If the you feel like the book can be improved in anyway please email me on kdp@tilcangroup.com and I will hopefully make things write :).

Your satisfaction is the number one priority!

Suggested books for you:

1: 'Mindfulness' - Top 10 Tips to Overcoming Obsessions and Compulsions Using Mindfulness

OCD is a mental disorder that causes people to have compulsions to do things repeatedly, such as washing their hands or checking to make sure that the door is locked. While some who have never experienced OCD may think of is as annoying or simply paranoia, it is actually harmful and, in extreme cases, can lead to suicide.

At the core of many cases of OCD is intense anxiety. This anxiety may be connected to a past traumatic event, ongoing stress, or even a genetic predisposition. The anxiety tends to be persistent and ongoing, with the person suffering rarely getting a break.

One of the best treatments for anxiety disorders, including OCD, is mindfulness. Mindfulness is the practice of constantly being aware of your own inner world and your environment in such a way that you are able to accept what is going on without being judgmental. Practicing mindfulness can actually alleviate some of the symptoms of OCD, helping people suffering from it get their lives back. This book will give you 10 different ways that you can practice mindfulness, with particular information as to how each of these different ways can benefit people with OCD.

This book is very easy to follow. It will guide you through practices such as deep breathing, meditation, journaling, being conscious of your surroundings, and slowing down a lifestyle that may actually be fueling anxiety. It includes self-reflective questions that will help you become more aware of your own anxiety, how it contributes to your OCD, and what practical steps you can take. Best of luck to you as you seek to become more

mindful and start to overcome your OCD.
Want to read further?
Simply click the country you are from below!

- I am from USA
- I am from UK
- I am from a different country

2: 'Airfryer Recipe' - For Quick and Healthy Meals

By purchasing the *Air Fryer Recipes for Quick and Healthy Meals*, you will soon be surprised how simple it really is to serve meals to your family that not only taste superb; they will improve your general health.

Leave all of the work to the Air Fryer. You can take the credit for the tasty dishes and no one has to know how you did it, unless you want to share.

These are just a few of the tempting recipes you will soon know how to prepare:

- Sausage Wraps
- Roast Turkey Reuben
- Meatloaf with Black Peppercorns
- Chicken Kiev Supper
- Lemon Fish
- Stuffed Mushrooms with Sour Cream
- Honey Roasted Carrot
- Avocado Fries

You will be using very little oil to prepare your dishes, since it works on the air theory. Think of all of the activities that can happen during the summer while the kids are out of school. Think of the time you can save if you already have a plan of a quick and healthy meal or snack. You are much more likely to encourage healthier eating habits when you don't have to spend hours cooking a meal. It is ready in no time!

You will discover these benefits when you start using your Air Fryer:

- The unit is a low-fat cooker. It is not necessary to use the extra oil as you normally would if you are using a deep fat fryer or skillet
- The fryer is fast and convenient to use whether it is day or night.
- You set the cooker and it automatically does the work for you. Set the buttons and enjoy your creation.
- The air fryer is easy to clean, and you won't need to clean the surrounding walls, floor, or counters since all of the oil vapors are held within the confines of the cooker. The only parts that need cleaning are the drip pan, cooking bowl or removable cooking basket.

If you want to start the journey to a healthier lifestyle; simply click which country, you are from below!

- I am from USA
- I am from UK
- I am from a different country

3: 'Vegan Slow Cooker Cookbook' - *Top 31 and Easy Slow Cooker Vegan Recipes*

You must see this to believe it! You will be surprised at the tasty treats that await you in the *Vegan Slow Cooker Cookbook: Top 31 Vegan Slow Cooker Recipes.*

Not only will you have a step by step guide, but it will also be simple to understand.

This is a sneak peek at what is in store if you decide to own your copy:

- Spiced Granola with Fruit and Nuts
- Spinach and Artichoke Pasta
- Italian Eggplant Casserole with Cashew-Tofu Ricotta
- Slow-Cooked Coconut Raisin Rice Pudding
- Cauliflower – Rice – Sushi Bowls with Tofu

These are some of the nutritional examples of how you will learn Vegan is a much healthier diet choice:

- Reduced saturated fats to improve cardiovascular health
- Carbs needed to keep from burning muscle tissue
- Healthier Protein Choices including nuts and grains

You know the best way to discover the full details, simply click the country you are from below:

- I am from USA
- I am from UK
- I am from a different country

2: 'Ketogenic Diet for Beginners' - The Step by Step Guide For Beginners, For Weight Loss

If I told you that your body had a natural system for burning fat that you simply weren't utilizing, would you believe me? Most people wouldn't. However, more and more people are coming around to this wonderful diet in what I like to call the low-carb revolution.

The purpose of the ketogenic diet is to retrain your body to run on better fuel. Rather than glucose, your body will learn to run on fat for fuel. Eating this way will place your body in a position wherein it primarily uses fat, rather than sugar for energy.

However, the ketogenic diet is focused on one key concept: *ketosis*. *Ketosis* is, to simply say, an alternative way that the body can burn fuel. When one is in a state of *ketosis*, then they are burning what are called *ketones* for energy, instead of *carbohydrates* like usual. Ketones can be generated from both the body's fat deposits and stores, as well as from ingested fat. This leads us to the first way that ketosis can benefit you: you'll be *less hungry*. We'll talk more about the simple mechanics of weight loss either, but for right now, just understand this: fats burn *slower* than carbs do, which means that you'll be a lot less hungry a lot less often.

Want to read further?
Simply click the country you are from below!

- I am from USA
- I am from UK
- I am from a different country

www.ingramcontent.com/pod-product-compliance
Lightning Source LLC
Chambersburg PA
CBHW030732180526
45157CB00008BA/3142